Tuesday

January 1st, 2019

I0511827

6 am	
7	
8	
9	
10	
11	
12 pm	
1	
2	
3	
4	
5	
6	
7	
8	

Today's Priorities:

To Do List:

Notes:

Wednesday

January 2nd, 2019

6 am	
7	
8	
9	
10	
11	
12 pm	
1	
2	
3	
4	
5	
6	
7	
8	

Today's Priorities:

To Do List:

Notes:

Thursday

January 3rd, 2019

Time	
6 am	
7	
8	
9	
10	
11	
12 pm	
1	
2	
3	
4	
5	
6	
7	
8	

Today's Priorities:

To Do List:

Notes:

Friday
January 4th, 2019

Time	
6 am	
7	
8	
9	
10	
11	
12 pm	
1	
2	
3	
4	
5	
6	
7	
8	

Today's Priorities:

To Do List:

Notes:

Saturday

January 5th, 2019

6 am	
7	
8	
9	
10	
11	
12 pm	
1	
2	
3	
4	
5	
6	
7	
8	

Today's Priorities:

To Do List:

Notes:

Sunday
January 6th, 2019

Time	
6 am	
7	
8	
9	
10	
11	
12 pm	
1	
2	
3	
4	
5	
6	
7	
8	

Today's Priorities:

To Do List:

Notes:

Monday

January 7th, 2019

6 am	
7	
8	
9	
10	
11	
12 pm	
1	
2	
3	
4	
5	
6	
7	
8	

Today's Priorities:

To Do List:

Notes:

Tuesday

January 8th, 2019

6 am	
7	
8	
9	
10	
11	
12 pm	
1	
2	
3	
4	
5	
6	
7	
8	

Today's Priorities:

To Do List:

Notes:

Wednesday

January 9th, 2019

6 am	
7	
8	
9	
10	
11	
12 pm	
1	
2	
3	
4	
5	
6	
7	
8	

Today's Priorities:

To Do List:

Notes:

Thursday
January 10th, 2019

6 am	
7	
8	
9	
10	
11	
12 pm	
1	
2	
3	
4	
5	
6	
7	
8	

Today's Priorities:

To Do List:

Notes:

Friday

January 11th, 2019

Time	
6 am	
7	
8	
9	
10	
11	
12 pm	
1	
2	
3	
4	
5	
6	
7	
8	

Today's Priorities:

To Do List:

Notes:

Saturday

January 12th, 2019

6 am	
7	
8	
9	
10	
11	
12 pm	
1	
2	
3	
4	
5	
6	
7	
8	

Today's Priorities:

To Do List:

Notes:

Sunday

January 13th, 2019

Time	
6 am	
7	
8	
9	
10	
11	
12 pm	
1	
2	
3	
4	
5	
6	
7	
8	

Today's Priorities:

To Do List:

Notes:

Monday

January 14th, 2019

6 am	
7	
8	
9	
10	
11	
12 pm	
1	
2	
3	
4	
5	
6	
7	
8	

Today's Priorities:

To Do List:

Notes:

Tuesday

January 15th, 2019

6 am	
7	
8	
9	
10	
11	
12 pm	
1	
2	
3	
4	
5	
6	
7	
8	

Today's Priorities:

To Do List:

Notes:

Wednesday

January 16th, 2019

6 am
7
8
9
10
11
12 pm
1
2
3
4
5
6
7
8

Notes:

Today's Priorities:

To Do List:

Thursday

January 17th, 2019

Time	
6 am	
7	
8	
9	
10	
11	
12 pm	
1	
2	
3	
4	
5	
6	
7	
8	

Today's Priorities:

To Do List:

Notes:

Friday
January 18th, 2019

6 am	
7	
8	
9	
10	
11	
12 pm	
1	
2	
3	
4	
5	
6	
7	
8	

Today's Priorities:
_____
_____
_____
_____
_____
_____

To Do List:
_____
_____
_____
_____
_____
_____
_____
_____
_____

Notes:
_____
_____
_____

Saturday

January 19th, 2019

6 am	
7	
8	
9	
10	
11	
12 pm	
1	
2	
3	
4	
5	
6	
7	
8	

Today's Priorities:

To Do List:

Notes:

Sunday

January 20th, 2019

6 am	
7	
8	
9	
10	
11	
12 pm	
1	
2	
3	
4	
5	
6	
7	
8	

Today's Priorities:

To Do List:

Notes:

Monday

January 21st, 2019

Time	
6 am	
7	
8	
9	
10	
11	
12 pm	
1	
2	
3	
4	
5	
6	
7	
8	

Today's Priorities:

To Do List:

Notes:

Tuesday
January 22nd, 2019

- 6 am
- 7
- 8
- 9
- 10
- 11
- 12 pm
- 1
- 2
- 3
- 4
- 5
- 6
- 7
- 8

Notes:

Today's Priorities:

To Do List:

Wednesday

January 23rd, 2019

6 am	
7	
8	
9	
10	
11	
12 pm	
1	
2	
3	
4	
5	
6	
7	
8	

Today's Priorities:

To Do List:

Notes:

Thursday

January 24th, 2019

6 am	
7	
8	
9	
10	
11	
12 pm	
1	
2	
3	
4	
5	
6	
7	
8	

Today's Priorities:

To Do List:

Notes:

Friday

January 25th, 2019

Time	
6 am	
7	
8	
9	
10	
11	
12 pm	
1	
2	
3	
4	
5	
6	
7	
8	

Today's Priorities:

To Do List:

Notes:

Saturday

January 26th, 2019

6 am	
7	
8	
9	
10	
11	
12 pm	
1	
2	
3	
4	
5	
6	
7	
8	

Today's Priorities:

To Do List:

Notes:

Sunday

January 27th, 2019

Time	
6 am	
7	
8	
9	
10	
11	
12 pm	
1	
2	
3	
4	
5	
6	
7	
8	

Today's Priorities:

To Do List:

Notes:

Monday
January 28th, 2019

6 am	
7	
8	
9	
10	
11	
12 pm	
1	
2	
3	
4	
5	
6	
7	
8	

Today's Priorities:

To Do List:

Notes:

Tuesday

January 29th, 2019

6 am	
7	
8	
9	
10	
11	
12 pm	
1	
2	
3	
4	
5	
6	
7	
8	

Today's Priorities:

To Do List:

Notes:

Wednesday
January 30th, 2019

- 6 am
- 7
- 8
- 9
- 10
- 11
- 12 pm
- 1
- 2
- 3
- 4
- 5
- 6
- 7
- 8

Today's Priorities:

To Do List:

Notes:

Thursday

January 31st, 2019

6 am	
7	
8	
9	
10	
11	
12 pm	
1	
2	
3	
4	
5	
6	
7	
8	

Today's Priorities:

To Do List:

Notes:

Friday
February 1st, 2019

Time	
6 am	
7	
8	
9	
10	
11	
12 pm	
1	
2	
3	
4	
5	
6	
7	
8	

Today's Priorities:

To Do List:

Notes:

Saturday
February 2nd, 2019

6 am	
7	
8	
9	
10	
11	
12 pm	
1	
2	
3	
4	
5	
6	
7	
8	

Today's Priorities:

To Do List:

Notes:

Sunday
February 3rd, 2019

6 am	
7	
8	
9	
10	
11	
12 pm	
1	
2	
3	
4	
5	
6	
7	
8	

Today's Priorities:

To Do List:

Notes:

Monday
February 4th, 2019

6 am	
7	
8	
9	
10	
11	
12 pm	
1	
2	
3	
4	
5	
6	
7	
8	

Today's Priorities:

To Do List:

Notes:

Tuesday

February 5th, 2019

6 am	
7	
8	
9	
10	
11	
12 pm	
1	
2	
3	
4	
5	
6	
7	
8	

Today's Priorities:

To Do List:

Notes:

Wednesday

February 6th, 2019

6 am	
7	
8	
9	
10	
11	
12 pm	
1	
2	
3	
4	
5	
6	
7	
8	

Today's Priorities:

To Do List:

Notes:

Thursday

February 7th, 2019

6 am	
7	
8	
9	
10	
11	
12 pm	
1	
2	
3	
4	
5	
6	
7	
8	

Today's Priorities:

To Do List:

Notes:

Friday

February 8th, 2019

6 am	
7	
8	
9	
10	
11	
12 pm	
1	
2	
3	
4	
5	
6	
7	
8	

Today's Priorities:

To Do List:

Notes:

Saturday
February 9th, 2019

Time	
6 am	
7	
8	
9	
10	
11	
12 pm	
1	
2	
3	
4	
5	
6	
7	
8	

Today's Priorities:

To Do List:

Notes:

Sunday

February 10th, 2019

Time	
6 am	
7	
8	
9	
10	
11	
12 pm	
1	
2	
3	
4	
5	
6	
7	
8	

Today's Priorities:

To Do List:

Notes:

Monday

February 11th, 2019

6 am	
7	
8	
9	
10	
11	
12 pm	
1	
2	
3	
4	
5	
6	
7	
8	

Today's Priorities:

To Do List:

Notes:

Tuesday

February 12th, 2019

6 am	
7	
8	Today's Priorities:
9	
10	
11	
12 pm	
1	To Do List:
2	
3	
4	
5	
6	
7	
8	

Notes:

Wednesday

February 13th, 2019

6 am	
7	
8	
9	
10	
11	
12 pm	
1	
2	
3	
4	
5	
6	
7	
8	

Today's Priorities:

To Do List:

Notes:

Thursday

February 14th, 2019

6 am	
7	
8	
9	
10	
11	
12 pm	
1	
2	
3	
4	
5	
6	
7	
8	

Today's Priorities:

To Do List:

Notes:

Friday

February 15th, 2019

6 am	
7	
8	
9	
10	
11	
12 pm	
1	
2	
3	
4	
5	
6	
7	
8	

Today's Priorities:

To Do List:

Notes:

Saturday

February 16th, 2019

Time	
6 am	
7	
8	
9	
10	
11	
12 pm	
1	
2	
3	
4	
5	
6	
7	
8	

Today's Priorities:

To Do List:

Notes:

Sunday

February 17th, 2019

6 am	
7	
8	
9	
10	
11	
12 pm	
1	
2	
3	
4	
5	
6	
7	
8	

Today's Priorities:

To Do List:

Notes:

Monday

February 18th, 2019

Time	
6 am	
7	
8	
9	
10	
11	
12 pm	
1	
2	
3	
4	
5	
6	
7	
8	

Today's Priorities:

To Do List:

Notes:

Tuesday

February 19th, 2019

6 am	
7	
8	
9	
10	
11	
12 pm	
1	
2	
3	
4	
5	
6	
7	
8	

Today's Priorities:

To Do List:

Notes:

Wednesday

February 20th, 2019

6 am	
7	
8	
9	
10	
11	
12 pm	
1	
2	
3	
4	
5	
6	
7	
8	

Today's Priorities:

To Do List:

Notes:

Thursday
February 21st, 2019

Time	
6 am	
7	
8	
9	
10	
11	
12 pm	
1	
2	
3	
4	
5	
6	
7	
8	

Today's Priorities:

To Do List:

Notes:

Friday

February 22nd, 2019

Time		
6 am		
7		Today's Priorities:
8		
9		
10		
11		
12 pm		
1		To Do List:
2		
3		
4		
5		
6		
7		
8		

Notes:

Saturday

February 23rd, 2019

Time
6 am
7
8
9
10
11
12 pm
1
2
3
4
5
6
7
8

Today's Priorities:

To Do List:

Notes:

Sunday

February 24th, 2019

6 am	
7	
8	Today's Priorities:
9	
10	
11	
12 pm	
1	To Do List:
2	
3	
4	
5	
6	
7	
8	

Notes:

Monday

February 25th, 2019

Time	
6 am	
7	
8	
9	
10	
11	
12 pm	
1	
2	
3	
4	
5	
6	
7	
8	

Today's Priorities:
_____
_____
_____
_____
_____

To Do List:
_____
_____
_____
_____
_____
_____
_____
_____
_____
_____

Notes:
_____
_____
_____
_____

Tuesday

February 26th, 2019

6 am	
7	
8	
9	
10	
11	
12 pm	
1	
2	
3	
4	
5	
6	
7	
8	

Today's Priorities:

To Do List:

Notes:

Wednesday

February 27th, 2019

6 am
7
8
9
10
11
12 pm
1
2
3
4
5
6
7
8

Notes:

Today's Priorities:

To Do List:

Thursday

February 28th, 2019

6 am	
7	
8	
9	
10	
11	
12 pm	
1	
2	
3	
4	
5	
6	
7	
8	

Today's Priorities:

To Do List:

Notes:

Friday
March 1st, 2019

6 am	
7	
8	
9	
10	
11	
12 pm	
1	
2	
3	
4	
5	
6	
7	
8	

Today's Priorities:

To Do List:

Notes:

Saturday

March 2nd, 2019

6 am	
7	
8	
9	
10	
11	
12 pm	
1	
2	
3	
4	
5	
6	
7	
8	

Today's Priorities:

To Do List:

Notes:

Sunday
March 3rd, 2019

6 am	
7	
8	
9	
10	
11	
12 pm	
1	
2	
3	
4	
5	
6	
7	
8	

Today's Priorities:

To Do List:

Notes:

Monday

March 4th, 2019

Time	
6 am	
7	
8	
9	
10	
11	
12 pm	
1	
2	
3	
4	
5	
6	
7	
8	

Today's Priorities:

To Do List:

Notes:

Tuesday

March 5th, 2019

Time	
6 am	
7	
8	
9	
10	
11	
12 pm	
1	
2	
3	
4	
5	
6	
7	
8	

Today's Priorities:

To Do List:

Notes:

Wednesday

March 6th, 2019

6 am	
7	
8	
9	**Today's Priorities:**
10	
11	
12 pm	
1	**To Do List:**
2	
3	
4	
5	
6	
7	
8	

Notes:

Thursday
March 7th, 2019

Time	
6 am	
7	
8	
9	
10	
11	
12 pm	
1	
2	
3	
4	
5	
6	
7	
8	

Today's Priorities:

To Do List:

Notes:

Friday

March 8th, 2019

6 am	
7	
8	
9	
10	
11	
12 pm	
1	
2	
3	
4	
5	
6	
7	
8	

Today's Priorities:

To Do List:

Notes:

Saturday

March 9th, 2019

6 am	
7	
8	
9	
10	
11	
12 pm	
1	
2	
3	
4	
5	
6	
7	
8	

Today's Priorities:

To Do List:

Notes:

Sunday

March 10th, 2019

6 am	
7	
8	
9	
10	
11	
12 pm	
1	
2	
3	
4	
5	
6	
7	
8	

Today's Priorities:

To Do List:

Notes:

Monday

March 11th, 2019

6 am	
7	
8	
9	
10	
11	
12 pm	
1	
2	
3	
4	
5	
6	
7	
8	

Today's Priorities:

To Do List:

Notes:

Tuesday

March 12th, 2019

6 am	
7	
8	
9	
10	
11	
12 pm	
1	
2	
3	
4	
5	
6	
7	
8	

Today's Priorities:

To Do List:

Notes:

Wednesday

March 13th, 2019

Time	
6 am	
7	
8	
9	
10	
11	
12 pm	
1	
2	
3	
4	
5	
6	
7	
8	

Today's Priorities:

To Do List:

Notes:

Thursday

March 14th, 2019

Time	
6 am	
7	
8	
9	
10	
11	
12 pm	
1	
2	
3	
4	
5	
6	
7	
8	

Today's Priorities:

To Do List:

Notes:

Friday
March 15th, 2019

6 am	
7	
8	
9	
10	
11	
12 pm	
1	
2	
3	
4	
5	
6	
7	
8	

Today's Priorities:

To Do List:

Notes:

Saturday

March 16th, 2019

Time	
6 am	
7	
8	
9	
10	
11	
12 pm	
1	
2	
3	
4	
5	
6	
7	
8	

Today's Priorities:

To Do List:

Notes:

Sunday

March 17th, 2019

6 am	
7	
8	
9	
10	
11	
12 pm	
1	
2	
3	
4	
5	
6	
7	
8	

Today's Priorities:

To Do List:

Notes:

Monday

March 18th, 2019

Time	
6 am	
7	
8	
9	
10	
11	
12 pm	
1	
2	
3	
4	
5	
6	
7	
8	

Today's Priorities:

To Do List:

Notes:

Tuesday

March 19th, 2019

6 am	
7	
8	
9	
10	
11	
12 pm	
1	
2	
3	
4	
5	
6	
7	
8	

Today's Priorities:

To Do List:

Notes:

Wednesday

March 20th, 2019

6 am	
7	
8	
9	
10	
11	
12 pm	
1	
2	
3	
4	
5	
6	
7	
8	

Today's Priorities:

To Do List:

Notes:

Thursday

March 21st, 2019

Time
6 am
7
8
9
10
11
12 pm
1
2
3
4
5
6
7
8

Today's Priorities:

To Do List:

Notes:

Friday

March 22nd, 2019

Time		
6 am		
7		Today's Priorities:
8		
9		
10		
11		
12 pm		
1		To Do List:
2		
3		
4		
5		
6		
7		
8		

Notes:

Saturday

March 23rd, 2019

Time	
6 am	
7	
8	
9	
10	
11	
12 pm	
1	
2	
3	
4	
5	
6	
7	
8	

Today's Priorities:

To Do List:

Notes:

Sunday

March 24th, 2019

6 am	
7	
8	**Today's Priorities:**
9	
10	
11	
12 pm	
1	**To Do List:**
2	
3	
4	
5	
6	
7	
8	

Notes:

Monday
March 25th, 2019

Time	
6 am	
7	
8	
9	
10	
11	
12 pm	
1	
2	
3	
4	
5	
6	
7	
8	

Today's Priorities:

To Do List:

Notes:

Tuesday

March 26th, 2019

6 am	
7	
8	
9	
10	
11	
12 pm	
1	
2	
3	
4	
5	
6	
7	
8	

Today's Priorities:

To Do List:

Notes:

Wednesday

March 27th, 2019

6 am
7
8
9
10
11
12 pm
1
2
3
4
5
6
7
8

Today's Priorities:

To Do List:

Notes:

Thursday

March 28th, 2019

6 am	
7	
8	
9	
10	
11	
12 pm	
1	
2	
3	
4	
5	
6	
7	
8	

Today's Priorities:

To Do List:

Notes:

Friday
March 29th, 2019

6 am	
7	
8	
9	
10	
11	
12 pm	
1	
2	
3	
4	
5	
6	
7	
8	

Today's Priorities:

To Do List:

Notes:

Saturday

March 30th, 2019

6 am	
7	
8	
9	
10	
11	
12 pm	
1	
2	
3	
4	
5	
6	
7	
8	

Today's Priorities:

To Do List:

Notes:

Sunday

March 31st, 2019

Time	
6 am	
7	
8	
9	
10	
11	
12 pm	
1	
2	
3	
4	
5	
6	
7	
8	

Today's Priorities:

To Do List:

Notes:

Monday

April 1st, 2019

Time	
6 am	
7	
8	
9	
10	
11	
12 pm	
1	
2	
3	
4	
5	
6	
7	
8	

Today's Priorities:

To Do List:

Notes:

Tuesday

April 2nd, 2019

6 am	
7	
8	
9	
10	
11	
12 pm	
1	
2	
3	
4	
5	
6	
7	
8	

Today's Priorities:

To Do List:

Notes:

Wednesday

April 3rd, 2019

Time	
6 am	
7	
8	
9	
10	
11	
12 pm	
1	
2	
3	
4	
5	
6	
7	
8	

Today's Priorities:

To Do List:

Notes:

Thursday

April 4th, 2019

6 am	
7	
8	
9	
10	
11	
12 pm	
1	
2	
3	
4	
5	
6	
7	
8	

Today's Priorities:

To Do List:

Notes:

Friday

April 5th, 2019

6 am	
7	
8	
9	
10	
11	
12 pm	
1	
2	
3	
4	
5	
6	
7	
8	

Today's Priorities:

To Do List:

Notes:

Saturday

April 6th, 2019

6 am	
7	
8	
9	
10	
11	
12 pm	
1	
2	
3	
4	
5	
6	
7	
8	

Today's Priorities:

To Do List:

Notes:

Sunday

April 7th, 2019

Time	
6 am	
7	
8	
9	
10	
11	
12 pm	
1	
2	
3	
4	
5	
6	
7	
8	

Today's Priorities:

To Do List:

Notes:

Monday

April 8th, 2019

6 am	
7	
8	
9	
10	
11	
12 pm	
1	
2	
3	
4	
5	
6	
7	
8	

Today's Priorities:

To Do List:

Notes:

Tuesday

April 9th, 2019

6 am	
7	
8	
9	
10	
11	
12 pm	
1	
2	
3	
4	
5	
6	
7	
8	

Today's Priorities:

To Do List:

Notes:

Wednesday

April 10th, 2019

6 am
7
8
9
10
11
12 pm
1
2
3
4
5
6
7
8

Today's Priorities:

To Do List:

Notes:

Thursday

April 11th, 2019

6 am	
7	
8	
9	
10	
11	
12 pm	
1	
2	
3	
4	
5	
6	
7	
8	

Today's Priorities:

To Do List:

Notes:

Friday

April 12th, 2019

- 6 am
- 7
- 8
- 9
- 10
- 11
- 12 pm
- 1
- 2
- 3
- 4
- 5
- 6
- 7
- 8

Today's Priorities:

To Do List:

Notes:

Saturday

April 13th, 2019

6 am	
7	
8	
9	
10	
11	
12 pm	
1	
2	
3	
4	
5	
6	
7	
8	

Today's Priorities:

To Do List:

Notes:

Sunday

April 14th, 2019

6 am	
7	
8	
9	
10	
11	
12 pm	
1	
2	
3	
4	
5	
6	
7	
8	

Today's Priorities:

To Do List:

Notes:

Monday

April 15th, 2019

6 am	
7	
8	
9	
10	
11	
12 pm	
1	
2	
3	
4	
5	
6	
7	
8	

Today's Priorities:

To Do List:

Notes:

Tuesday

April 16th, 2019

6 am	
7	
8	
9	
10	
11	
12 pm	
1	
2	
3	
4	
5	
6	
7	
8	

Today's Priorities:

To Do List:

Notes:

Wednesday

April 17th, 2019

6 am	
7	
8	
9	**Today's Priorities:**
10	
11	
12 pm	
1	**To Do List:**
2	
3	
4	
5	
6	
7	
8	

Notes:

Thursday

April 18th, 2019

6 am	
7	
8	
9	
10	
11	
12 pm	
1	
2	
3	
4	
5	
6	
7	
8	

Today's Priorities:

To Do List:

Notes:

Friday

April 19th, 2019

Time	
6 am	
7	
8	
9	
10	
11	
12 pm	
1	
2	
3	
4	
5	
6	
7	
8	

Today's Priorities:

To Do List:

Notes:

Saturday

April 20th, 2019

6 am	
7	
8	
9	
10	
11	
12 pm	
1	
2	
3	
4	
5	
6	
7	
8	

Today's Priorities:

To Do List:

Notes:

Sunday

April 21st, 2019

Time	
6 am	
7	
8	
9	
10	
11	
12 pm	
1	
2	
3	
4	
5	
6	
7	
8	

Today's Priorities:

To Do List:

Notes:

Monday

April 22nd, 2019

Time	
6 am	
7	
8	
9	
10	
11	
12 pm	
1	
2	
3	
4	
5	
6	
7	
8	

Today's Priorities:

To Do List:

Notes:

Tuesday

April 23rd, 2019

6 am	
7	
8	
9	
10	
11	
12 pm	
1	
2	
3	
4	
5	
6	
7	
8	

Today's Priorities:

To Do List:

Notes:

Wednesday

April 24th, 2019

6 am	
7	
8	
9	
10	
11	
12 pm	
1	
2	
3	
4	
5	
6	
7	
8	

Today's Priorities:

To Do List:

Notes:

Thursday

April 25th, 2019

6 am	
7	
8	
9	
10	
11	
12 pm	
1	
2	
3	
4	
5	
6	
7	
8	

Today's Priorities:

To Do List:

Notes:

Friday

April 26th, 2019

6 am	
7	
8	
9	
10	
11	
12 pm	
1	
2	
3	
4	
5	
6	
7	
8	

Today's Priorities:

To Do List:

Notes:

Saturday

April 27th, 2019

6 am	
7	
8	
9	
10	
11	
12 pm	
1	
2	
3	
4	
5	
6	
7	
8	

Today's Priorities:

To Do List:

Notes:

Sunday

April 28th, 2019

6 am	
7	
8	
9	
10	
11	
12 pm	
1	
2	
3	
4	
5	
6	
7	
8	

Today's Priorities:

To Do List:

Notes:

Monday

April 29th, 2019

Time	
6 am	
7	
8	
9	
10	
11	
12 pm	
1	
2	
3	
4	
5	
6	
7	
8	

Today's Priorities:

To Do List:

Notes:

Tuesday

April 30th, 2019

6 am	
7	
8	
9	
10	
11	
12 pm	
1	
2	
3	
4	
5	
6	
7	
8	

Today's Priorities:

To Do List:

Notes:

Wednesday

May 1st, 2019

Time	
6 am	
7	
8	
9	
10	
11	
12 pm	
1	
2	
3	
4	
5	
6	
7	
8	

Today's Priorities:

To Do List:

Notes:

Thursday

May 2nd, 2019

6 am	
7	
8	
9	
10	
11	
12 pm	
1	
2	
3	
4	
5	
6	
7	
8	

Today's Priorities:

To Do List:

Notes:

Friday

May 3rd, 2019

6 am	
7	
8	
9	
10	
11	
12 pm	
1	
2	
3	
4	
5	
6	
7	
8	

Today's Priorities:

To Do List:

Notes:

Saturday

May 4th, 2019

6 am	
7	
8	
9	
10	
11	
12 pm	
1	
2	
3	
4	
5	
6	
7	
8	

Today's Priorities:

To Do List:

Notes:

Sunday

May 5th, 2019

6 am	
7	
8	
9	
10	
11	
12 pm	
1	
2	
3	
4	
5	
6	
7	
8	

Today's Priorities:

To Do List:

Notes:

Monday

May 6th, 2019

6 am	
7	
8	
9	
10	
11	
12 pm	
1	
2	
3	
4	
5	
6	
7	
8	

Today's Priorities:

To Do List:

Notes:

Tuesday

May 7th, 2019

- 6 am
- 7
- 8
- 9
- 10
- 11
- 12 pm
- 1
- 2
- 3
- 4
- 5
- 6
- 7
- 8

Today's Priorities:

To Do List:

Notes:

Wednesday

May 8th, 2019

6 am	
7	
8	
9	
10	
11	
12 pm	
1	
2	
3	
4	
5	
6	
7	
8	

Today's Priorities:

To Do List:

Notes:

Thursday

May 9th, 2019

6 am	
7	
8	
9	
10	
11	
12 pm	
1	
2	
3	
4	
5	
6	
7	
8	

Today's Priorities:

To Do List:

Notes:

Friday

May 10th, 2019

Time	
6 am	
7	
8	
9	
10	
11	
12 pm	
1	
2	
3	
4	
5	
6	
7	
8	

Today's Priorities:

To Do List:

Notes:

Saturday

May 11th, 2019

6 am	
7	
8	
9	
10	
11	
12 pm	
1	
2	
3	
4	
5	
6	
7	
8	

Today's Priorities:

To Do List:

Notes:

Sunday

May 12th, 2019

Time	
6 am	
7	
8	
9	
10	
11	
12 pm	
1	
2	
3	
4	
5	
6	
7	
8	

Today's Priorities:

To Do List:

Notes:

Monday

May 13th, 2019

Time	
6 am	
7	
8	
9	
10	
11	
12 pm	
1	
2	
3	
4	
5	
6	
7	
8	

Today's Priorities:

To Do List:

Notes:

Tuesday

May 14th, 2019

6 am	
7	
8	
9	
10	
11	
12 pm	
1	
2	
3	
4	
5	
6	
7	
8	

Today's Priorities:

To Do List:

Notes:

Wednesday

May 15th, 2019

---

6 am
7
8
9
10
11
12 pm
1
2
3
4
5
6
7
8

Today's Priorities:

To Do List:

Notes:

Thursday
May 16th, 2019

- 6 am
- 7
- 8
- 9
- 10
- 11
- 12 pm
- 1
- 2
- 3
- 4
- 5
- 6
- 7
- 8

Today's Priorities:

To Do List:

Notes:

Friday

May 17th, 2019

6 am	
7	
8	
9	
10	
11	
12 pm	
1	
2	
3	
4	
5	
6	
7	
8	

Today's Priorities:

To Do List:

Notes:

Saturday

May 18th, 2019

Time	
6 am	
7	
8	
9	
10	
11	
12 pm	
1	
2	
3	
4	
5	
6	
7	
8	

Today's Priorities:

To Do List:

Notes:

Sunday

May 19th, 2019

Time	
6 am	
7	
8	
9	
10	
11	
12 pm	
1	
2	
3	
4	
5	
6	
7	
8	

Today's Priorities:

To Do List:

Notes:

Monday
May 20th, 2019

6 am	
7	
8	
9	
10	
11	
12 pm	
1	
2	
3	
4	
5	
6	
7	
8	

Today's Priorities:

To Do List:

Notes:

Tuesday

May 21st, 2019

6 am	
7	
8	
9	
10	
11	
12 pm	
1	
2	
3	
4	
5	
6	
7	
8	

Today's Priorities:

To Do List:

Notes:

Wednesday

May 22nd, 2019

6 am	
7	
8	
9	
10	
11	
12 pm	
1	
2	
3	
4	
5	
6	
7	
8	

Today's Priorities:

To Do List:

Notes:

Thursday

May 23rd, 2019

6 am	
7	
8	
9	
10	
11	
12 pm	
1	
2	
3	
4	
5	
6	
7	
8	

Today's Priorities:

To Do List:

Notes:

Friday

May 24th, 2019

6 am	
7	
8	
9	
10	
11	
12 pm	
1	
2	
3	
4	
5	
6	
7	
8	

Today's Priorities:

To Do List:

Notes:

Saturday

May 25th, 2019

6 am
7
8
9
10
11
12 pm
1
2
3
4
5
6
7
8

Today's Priorities:

To Do List:

Notes:

Sunday
May 26th, 2019

6 am	
7	
8	
9	
10	
11	
12 pm	
1	
2	
3	
4	
5	
6	
7	
8	

Today's Priorities:

To Do List:

Notes:

Monday

May 27th, 2019

Time	
6 am	
7	
8	
9	
10	
11	
12 pm	
1	
2	
3	
4	
5	
6	
7	
8	

Today's Priorities:

To Do List:

Notes:

Tuesday

May 28th, 2019

6 am	
7	
8	
9	
10	
11	
12 pm	
1	
2	
3	
4	
5	
6	
7	
8	

Today's Priorities:

To Do List:

Notes:

Wednesday

May 29th, 2019

6 am	
7	
8	
9	
10	
11	
12 pm	
1	
2	
3	
4	
5	
6	
7	
8	

Today's Priorities:

To Do List:

Notes:

Thursday
May 30th, 2019

Time	
6 am	
7	
8	
9	
10	
11	
12 pm	
1	
2	
3	
4	
5	
6	
7	
8	

Today's Priorities:

To Do List:

Notes:

Friday
May 31st, 2019

Time	
6 am	
7	
8	
9	
10	
11	
12 pm	
1	
2	
3	
4	
5	
6	
7	
8	

Today's Priorities:

To Do List:

Notes:

Saturday

June 1st, 2019

6 am	
7	
8	
9	
10	
11	
12 pm	
1	
2	
3	
4	
5	
6	
7	
8	

Today's Priorities:

To Do List:

Notes:

Sunday

June 2nd, 2019

6 am	
7	
8	
9	
10	
11	
12 pm	
1	
2	
3	
4	
5	
6	
7	
8	

Today's Priorities:

To Do List:

Notes:

Monday

June 3rd, 2019

6 am	
7	
8	
9	
10	
11	
12 pm	
1	
2	
3	
4	
5	
6	
7	
8	

Today's Priorities:

To Do List:

Notes:

Tuesday

June 4th, 2019

6 am	
7	
8	
9	
10	
11	
12 pm	
1	
2	
3	
4	
5	
6	
7	
8	

Today's Priorities:

To Do List:

Notes:

Wednesday

June 5th, 2019

6 am	
7	
8	
9	
10	
11	
12 pm	
1	
2	
3	
4	
5	
6	
7	
8	

Today's Priorities:

To Do List:

Notes:

Thursday

June 6th, 2019

6 am	
7	
8	
9	
10	
11	
12 pm	
1	
2	
3	
4	
5	
6	
7	
8	

Today's Priorities:

To Do List:

Notes:

Friday
June 7th, 2019

6 am	
7	
8	
9	
10	
11	
12 pm	
1	
2	
3	
4	
5	
6	
7	
8	

Today's Priorities:

To Do List:

Notes:

Saturday

June 8th, 2019

6 am	
7	
8	
9	
10	
11	
12 pm	
1	
2	
3	
4	
5	
6	
7	
8	

Today's Priorities:

To Do List:

Notes:

Sunday
June 9th, 2019

6 am	
7	
8	
9	
10	
11	
12 pm	
1	
2	
3	
4	
5	
6	
7	
8	

Today's Priorities:
_____
_____
_____
_____
_____

To Do List:
_____
_____
_____
_____
_____
_____
_____
_____
_____

Notes:
_____
_____
_____

Monday

June 10th, 2019

6 am	
7	
8	
9	
10	
11	
12 pm	
1	
2	
3	
4	
5	
6	
7	
8	

Today's Priorities:

To Do List:

Notes:

Tuesday

June 11th, 2019

6 am	
7	
8	
9	
10	
11	
12 pm	
1	
2	
3	
4	
5	
6	
7	
8	

Today's Priorities:

To Do List:

Notes:

Wednesday

June 12th, 2019

Time	
6 am	
7	
8	
9	
10	
11	
12 pm	
1	
2	
3	
4	
5	
6	
7	
8	

Today's Priorities:

To Do List:

Notes:

Thursday

June 13th, 2019

6 am	
7	
8	
9	
10	
11	
12 pm	
1	
2	
3	
4	
5	
6	
7	
8	

Today's Priorities:

To Do List:

Notes:

Friday

June 14th, 2019

Time	
6 am	
7	
8	
9	
10	
11	
12 pm	
1	
2	
3	
4	
5	
6	
7	
8	

Today's Priorities:

To Do List:

Notes:

Saturday
June 15th, 2019

Time	
6 am	
7	
8	
9	
10	
11	
12 pm	
1	
2	
3	
4	
5	
6	
7	
8	

Today's Priorities:

To Do List:

Notes:

Sunday

June 16th, 2019

Time	
6 am	
7	
8	
9	
10	
11	
12 pm	
1	
2	
3	
4	
5	
6	
7	
8	

Today's Priorities:

To Do List:

Notes:

Monday

June 17th, 2019

6 am	
7	
8	
9	
10	
11	
12 pm	
1	
2	
3	
4	
5	
6	
7	
8	

Today's Priorities:

To Do List:

Notes:

Tuesday

June 18th, 2019

6 am	
7	
8	
9	
10	
11	
12 pm	
1	
2	
3	
4	
5	
6	
7	
8	

Today's Priorities:

To Do List:

Notes:

Wednesday

June 19th, 2019

6 am
7
8
9
10
11
12 pm
1
2
3
4
5
6
7
8

Today's Priorities:

To Do List:

Notes:

Thursday

June 20th, 2019

6 am	
7	
8	
9	
10	
11	
12 pm	
1	
2	
3	
4	
5	
6	
7	
8	

Today's Priorities:

To Do List:

Notes:

Friday

June 21st, 2019

6 am	
7	
8	
9	
10	
11	
12 pm	
1	
2	
3	
4	
5	
6	
7	
8	

Today's Priorities:

To Do List:

Notes:

Saturday

June 22nd, 2019

6 am	
7	
8	
9	
10	
11	
12 pm	
1	
2	
3	
4	
5	
6	
7	
8	

Today's Priorities:

To Do List:

Notes:

Sunday

June 23rd, 2019

6 am	
7	
8	
9	
10	
11	
12 pm	
1	
2	
3	
4	
5	
6	
7	
8	

Today's Priorities:

To Do List:

Notes:

Monday
June 24th, 2019

6 am	
7	
8	**Today's Priorities:**
9	
10	
11	
12 pm	
1	**To Do List:**
2	
3	
4	
5	
6	
7	
8	

Notes:

Tuesday

June 25th, 2019

6 am	
7	
8	
9	
10	
11	
12 pm	
1	
2	
3	
4	
5	
6	
7	
8	

Today's Priorities:

To Do List:

Notes:

Wednesday

June 26th, 2019

6 am	
7	
8	
9	
10	
11	
12 pm	
1	
2	
3	
4	
5	
6	
7	
8	

Today's Priorities:

To Do List:

Notes:

Thursday
June 27th, 2019

6 am	
7	
8	
9	
10	
11	
12 pm	
1	
2	
3	
4	
5	
6	
7	
8	

Today's Priorities:

To Do List:

Notes:

Friday

June 28th, 2019

6 am	
7	
8	
9	
10	
11	
12 pm	
1	
2	
3	
4	
5	
6	
7	
8	

Today's Priorities:

To Do List:

Notes:

Saturday

June 29th, 2019

6 am	
7	
8	
9	
10	
11	
12 pm	
1	
2	
3	
4	
5	
6	
7	
8	

Today's Priorities:

To Do List:

Notes:

Sunday

June 30th, 2019

6 am	
7	
8	
9	
10	
11	
12 pm	
1	
2	
3	
4	
5	
6	
7	
8	

Today's Priorities:

To Do List:

Notes:

Monday
July 1st, 2019

6 am
7
8
9
10
11
12 pm
1
2
3
4
5
6
7
8

Today's Priorities:

To Do List:

Notes:

Tuesday

July 2nd, 2019

6 am	
7	
8	
9	
10	
11	
12 pm	
1	
2	
3	
4	
5	
6	
7	
8	

Today's Priorities:

To Do List:

Notes:

Wednesday

July 3rd, 2019

6 am	
7	
8	
9	
10	
11	
12 pm	
1	
2	
3	
4	
5	
6	
7	
8	

Today's Priorities:

To Do List:

Notes:

Thursday

July 4th, 2019

6 am	
7	
8	
9	
10	
11	
12 pm	
1	
2	
3	
4	
5	
6	
7	
8	

Today's Priorities:

To Do List:

Notes:

Friday
July 5th, 2019

Time	
6 am	
7	
8	
9	
10	
11	
12 pm	
1	
2	
3	
4	
5	
6	
7	
8	

Today's Priorities:

To Do List:

Notes:

Saturday

July 6th, 2019

Time	
6 am	
7	
8	
9	
10	
11	
12 pm	
1	
2	
3	
4	
5	
6	
7	
8	

Today's Priorities:

To Do List:

Notes:

Sunday

July 7th, 2019

6 am	
7	
8	
9	
10	
11	
12 pm	
1	
2	
3	
4	
5	
6	
7	
8	

Today's Priorities:

To Do List:

Notes:

Monday

July 8th, 2019

6 am	
7	
8	
9	
10	
11	
12 pm	
1	
2	
3	
4	
5	
6	
7	
8	

Today's Priorities:

To Do List:

Notes:

Tuesday

July 9th, 2019

Time	
6 am	
7	
8	
9	
10	
11	
12 pm	
1	
2	
3	
4	
5	
6	
7	
8	

Today's Priorities:

To Do List:

Notes:

Wednesday

July 10th, 2019

Time	
6 am	
7	
8	
9	
10	
11	
12 pm	
1	
2	
3	
4	
5	
6	
7	
8	

Today's Priorities:

To Do List:

Notes:

Thursday
July 11th, 2019

Time	
6 am	
7	
8	
9	
10	
11	
12 pm	
1	
2	
3	
4	
5	
6	
7	
8	

Today's Priorities:

To Do List:

Notes:

Friday

July 12th, 2019

6 am	
7	
8	
9	
10	
11	
12 pm	
1	
2	
3	
4	
5	
6	
7	
8	

Today's Priorities:

To Do List:

Notes:

Saturday

July 13th, 2019

6 am	
7	
8	
9	
10	
11	
12 pm	
1	
2	
3	
4	
5	
6	
7	
8	

Today's Priorities:

To Do List:

Notes:

Sunday

July 14th, 2019

6 am	
7	
8	
9	
10	
11	
12 pm	
1	
2	
3	
4	
5	
6	
7	
8	

Today's Priorities:

To Do List:

Notes:

Monday
July 15th, 2019

6 am	
7	
8	
9	
10	
11	
12 pm	
1	
2	
3	
4	
5	
6	
7	
8	

Today's Priorities:

To Do List:

Notes:

Tuesday

July 16th, 2019

Time	
6 am	
7	
8	
9	
10	
11	
12 pm	
1	
2	
3	
4	
5	
6	
7	
8	

Today's Priorities:

To Do List:

Notes:

Wednesday

July 17th, 2019

Time	
6 am	
7	
8	
9	
10	
11	
12 pm	
1	
2	
3	
4	
5	
6	
7	
8	

Today's Priorities:

To Do List:

Notes:

Thursday

July 18th, 2019

6 am	
7	
8	
9	
10	
11	
12 pm	
1	
2	
3	
4	
5	
6	
7	
8	

Today's Priorities:

To Do List:

Notes:

Friday

July 19th, 2019

6 am	
7	
8	
9	
10	
11	
12 pm	
1	
2	
3	
4	
5	
6	
7	
8	

Today's Priorities:

To Do List:

Notes:

Saturday
July 20th, 2019

Time	
6 am	
7	
8	
9	
10	
11	
12 pm	
1	
2	
3	
4	
5	
6	
7	
8	

Today's Priorities:

To Do List:

Notes:

Sunday
July 21st, 2019

Time	
6 am	
7	
8	
9	
10	
11	
12 pm	
1	
2	
3	
4	
5	
6	
7	
8	

Today's Priorities:

To Do List:

Notes:

Monday

July 22nd, 2019

Time	
6 am	
7	
8	
9	
10	
11	
12 pm	
1	
2	
3	
4	
5	
6	
7	
8	

Today's Priorities:

To Do List:

Notes:

Tuesday

July 23rd, 2019

6 am	
7	
8	
9	
10	
11	
12 pm	
1	
2	
3	
4	
5	
6	
7	
8	

Today's Priorities:

To Do List:

Notes:

Wednesday

July 24th, 2019

Time	
6 am	
7	
8	
9	
10	
11	
12 pm	
1	
2	
3	
4	
5	
6	
7	
8	

Today's Priorities:

To Do List:

Notes:

Thursday

July 25th, 2019

Time	
6 am	
7	
8	
9	
10	
11	
12 pm	
1	
2	
3	
4	
5	
6	
7	
8	

Today's Priorities:

To Do List:

Notes:

Friday

July 26th, 2019

6 am	
7	
8	
9	
10	
11	
12 pm	
1	
2	
3	
4	
5	
6	
7	
8	

Today's Priorities:

To Do List:

Notes:

Saturday

July 27th, 2019

Time	
6 am	
7	
8	
9	
10	
11	
12 pm	
1	
2	
3	
4	
5	
6	
7	
8	

Today's Priorities:

To Do List:

Notes:

Sunday

July 28th, 2019

6 am	
7	Today's Priorities:
8	
9	
10	
11	
12 pm	
1	To Do List:
2	
3	
4	
5	
6	
7	
8	

Notes:

Monday

July 29th, 2019

Time	
6 am	
7	
8	
9	
10	
11	
12 pm	
1	
2	
3	
4	
5	
6	
7	
8	

Notes:

Today's Priorities:

To Do List:

Tuesday

July 30th, 2019

Time	
6 am	
7	
8	
9	
10	
11	
12 pm	
1	
2	
3	
4	
5	
6	
7	
8	

Today's Priorities:

To Do List:

Notes:

Wednesday
July 31st, 2019

6 am	
7	
8	
9	
10	
11	
12 pm	
1	
2	
3	
4	
5	
6	
7	
8	

Today's Priorities:

To Do List:

Notes:

Thursday

August 1st, 2019

Time	
6 am	
7	
8	
9	
10	
11	
12 pm	
1	
2	
3	
4	
5	
6	
7	
8	

Today's Priorities:

To Do List:

Notes:

Friday

August 2nd, 2019

Time	
6 am	
7	
8	
9	
10	
11	
12 pm	
1	
2	
3	
4	
5	
6	
7	
8	

Today's Priorities:

To Do List:

Notes:

Saturday

August 3rd, 2019

6 am	
7	
8	
9	
10	
11	
12 pm	
1	
2	
3	
4	
5	
6	
7	
8	

Today's Priorities:

To Do List:

Notes:

Sunday

August 4th, 2019

Time	
6 am	
7	
8	
9	
10	
11	
12 pm	
1	
2	
3	
4	
5	
6	
7	
8	

Today's Priorities:

To Do List:

Notes:

Monday

August 5th, 2019

Time	
6 am	
7	
8	
9	
10	
11	
12 pm	
1	
2	
3	
4	
5	
6	
7	
8	

Today's Priorities:

To Do List:

Notes:

Tuesday

August 6th, 2019

Time	
6 am	
7	
8	
9	
10	
11	
12 pm	
1	
2	
3	
4	
5	
6	
7	
8	

Today's Priorities:

To Do List:

Notes:

Wednesday

August 7th, 2019

Time	
6 am	
7	
8	
9	
10	
11	
12 pm	
1	
2	
3	
4	
5	
6	
7	
8	

Today's Priorities:

To Do List:

Notes:

Thursday

August 8th, 2019

- 6 am
- 7
- 8
- 9
- 10
- 11
- 12 pm
- 1
- 2
- 3
- 4
- 5
- 6
- 7
- 8

Notes:

Today's Priorities:

To Do List:

Friday

August 9th, 2019

6 am	
7	
8	
9	
10	
11	
12 pm	
1	
2	
3	
4	
5	
6	
7	
8	

Today's Priorities:

To Do List:

Notes:

Saturday

August 10th, 2019

- 6 am
- 7
- 8
- 9
- 10
- 11
- 12 pm
- 1
- 2
- 3
- 4
- 5
- 6
- 7
- 8

Notes:

Today's Priorities:

To Do List:

Sunday

August 11th, 2019

Time		Today's Priorities:
6 am		
7		
8		
9		
10		
11		
12 pm		To Do List:
1		
2		
3		
4		
5		
6		
7		
8		

Notes:

Monday

August 12th, 2019

6 am	
7	
8	
9	
10	
11	
12 pm	
1	
2	
3	
4	
5	
6	
7	
8	

Today's Priorities:

To Do List:

Notes:

Tuesday
August 13th, 2019

6 am	
7	
8	
9	
10	
11	
12 pm	
1	
2	
3	
4	
5	
6	
7	
8	

Today's Priorities:

To Do List:

Notes:

Wednesday

August 14th, 2019

6 am	
7	
8	
9	
10	
11	
12 pm	
1	
2	
3	
4	
5	
6	
7	
8	

Today's Priorities:

To Do List:

Notes:

Thursday

August 15th, 2019

Time	
6 am	
7	
8	
9	
10	
11	
12 pm	
1	
2	
3	
4	
5	
6	
7	
8	

Today's Priorities:

To Do List:

Notes:

Friday

August 16th, 2019

Time	
6 am	
7	
8	
9	
10	
11	
12 pm	
1	
2	
3	
4	
5	
6	
7	
8	

Today's Priorities:

To Do List:

Notes:

Saturday

August 17th, 2019

Time	
6 am	
7	
8	
9	
10	
11	
12 pm	
1	
2	
3	
4	
5	
6	
7	
8	

Today's Priorities:

To Do List:

Notes:

Sunday

August 18th, 2019

6 am	
7	
8	
9	
10	
11	
12 pm	
1	
2	
3	
4	
5	
6	
7	
8	

Today's Priorities:

To Do List:

Notes:

Monday

August 19th, 2019

6 am	
7	
8	
9	
10	
11	
12 pm	
1	
2	
3	
4	
5	
6	
7	
8	

Today's Priorities:

To Do List:

Notes:

Tuesday

August 20th, 2019

6 am	
7	
8	
9	
10	
11	
12 pm	
1	
2	
3	
4	
5	
6	
7	
8	

Today's Priorities:
_____
_____
_____
_____
_____

To Do List:
_____
_____
_____
_____
_____
_____
_____
_____
_____

Notes:
_____
_____
_____

Wednesday

August 21st, 2019

6 am	
7	
8	
9	
10	
11	
12 pm	
1	
2	
3	
4	
5	
6	
7	
8	

Today's Priorities:

To Do List:

Notes:

Thursday

August 22nd, 2019

6 am	
7	
8	
9	
10	
11	
12 pm	
1	
2	
3	
4	
5	
6	
7	
8	

Today's Priorities:

To Do List:

Notes:

Friday
August 23rd, 2019

Time	
6 am	
7	
8	
9	
10	
11	
12 pm	
1	
2	
3	
4	
5	
6	
7	
8	

Today's Priorities:

To Do List:

Notes:

Saturday

August 24th, 2019

6 am	
7	
8	
9	
10	
11	
12 pm	
1	
2	
3	
4	
5	
6	
7	
8	

Today's Priorities:

To Do List:

Notes:

Sunday

August 25th, 2019

Time	
6 am	
7	
8	
9	
10	
11	
12 pm	
1	
2	
3	
4	
5	
6	
7	
8	

Today's Priorities:

To Do List:

Notes:

Monday

August 26th, 2019

Time	
6 am	
7	
8	
9	
10	
11	
12 pm	
1	
2	
3	
4	
5	
6	
7	
8	

Today's Priorities:
_____
_____
_____
_____
_____

To Do List:
_____
_____
_____
_____
_____
_____
_____
_____
_____
_____

Notes:
_____
_____
_____

Tuesday

August 27th, 2019

6 am	
7	
8	
9	
10	
11	
12 pm	
1	
2	
3	
4	
5	
6	
7	
8	

Today's Priorities:

To Do List:

Notes:

Wednesday

August 28th, 2019

Time	
6 am	
7	
8	
9	
10	
11	
12 pm	
1	
2	
3	
4	
5	
6	
7	
8	

Today's Priorities:

To Do List:

Notes:

Thursday
August 29th, 2019

6 am	
7	
8	
9	
10	
11	
12 pm	
1	
2	
3	
4	
5	
6	
7	
8	

Today's Priorities:

To Do List:

Notes:

Friday
August 30th, 2019

6 am	
7	
8	
9	
10	
11	
12 pm	
1	
2	
3	
4	
5	
6	
7	
8	

Today's Priorities:

To Do List:

Notes:

Saturday

August 31st, 2019

6 am	
7	
8	
9	
10	
11	
12 pm	
1	
2	
3	
4	
5	
6	
7	
8	

Today's Priorities:

To Do List:

Notes:

Sunday
September 1st, 2019

6 am	
7	
8	
9	
10	
11	
12 pm	
1	
2	
3	
4	
5	
6	
7	
8	

Today's Priorities:

To Do List:

Notes:

Monday
September 2nd, 2019

6 am	
7	
8	
9	**Today's Priorities:**
10	
11	
12 pm	
1	**To Do List:**
2	
3	
4	
5	
6	
7	
8	

Notes:

Tuesday

September 3rd, 2019

6 am	
7	
8	
9	
10	
11	
12 pm	
1	
2	
3	
4	
5	
6	
7	
8	

Today's Priorities:

To Do List:

Notes:

Wednesday

September 4th, 2019

6 am	
7	
8	
9	
10	
11	
12 pm	
1	
2	
3	
4	
5	
6	
7	
8	

Today's Priorities:

To Do List:

Notes:

Thursday
September 5th, 2019

Time	
6 am	
7	
8	
9	
10	
11	
12 pm	
1	
2	
3	
4	
5	
6	
7	
8	

Today's Priorities:

To Do List:

Notes:

Friday
September 6th, 2019

Time	
6 am	
7	
8	
9	
10	
11	
12 pm	
1	
2	
3	
4	
5	
6	
7	
8	

Today's Priorities:

To Do List:

Notes:

Saturday

September 7th, 2019

6 am	
7	
8	
9	
10	
11	
12 pm	
1	
2	
3	
4	
5	
6	
7	
8	

Today's Priorities:

To Do List:

Notes:

Sunday
September 8th, 2019

6 am	
7	
8	
9	
10	
11	
12 pm	
1	
2	
3	
4	
5	
6	
7	
8	

Today's Priorities:

To Do List:

Notes:

Monday
September 9th, 2019

Time	
6 am	
7	
8	
9	
10	
11	
12 pm	
1	
2	
3	
4	
5	
6	
7	
8	

Today's Priorities:

To Do List:

Notes:

Tuesday

September 10th, 2019

6 am	
7	
8	
9	Today's Priorities:
10	
11	
12 pm	
1	To Do List:
2	
3	
4	
5	
6	
7	
8	

Notes:

Wednesday

September 11th, 2019

6 am	
7	
8	
9	
10	
11	
12 pm	
1	
2	
3	
4	
5	
6	
7	
8	

Today's Priorities:

To Do List:

Notes:

Thursday

September 12th, 2019

Time	
6 am	
7	
8	
9	
10	
11	
12 pm	
1	
2	
3	
4	
5	
6	
7	
8	

Today's Priorities:

To Do List:

Notes:

Friday
September 13th, 2019

6 am	
7	
8	
9	
10	
11	
12 pm	
1	
2	
3	
4	
5	
6	
7	
8	

Today's Priorities:
_____
_____
_____
_____
_____

To Do List:
_____
_____
_____
_____
_____
_____
_____
_____
_____

Notes:
_____
_____
_____

Saturday

September 14th, 2019

6 am	
7	
8	
9	
10	
11	
12 pm	
1	
2	
3	
4	
5	
6	
7	
8	

Today's Priorities:

To Do List:

Notes:

Sunday
September 15th, 2019

Time		
6 am		Today's Priorities:
7		
8		
9		
10		
11		
12 pm		
1		To Do List:
2		
3		
4		
5		
6		
7		
8		

Notes:

Monday

September 16th, 2019

6 am	
7	
8	
9	
10	
11	
12 pm	
1	
2	
3	
4	
5	
6	
7	
8	

Today's Priorities:

To Do List:

Notes:

Tuesday

September 17th, 2019

6 am	
7	
8	
9	
10	
11	
12 pm	
1	
2	
3	
4	
5	
6	
7	
8	

Today's Priorities:

To Do List:

Notes:

Wednesday

September 18th, 2019

6 am	
7	
8	
9	
10	
11	
12 pm	
1	
2	
3	
4	
5	
6	
7	
8	

Today's Priorities:

To Do List:

Notes:

Thursday

September 19th, 2019

6 am	
7	
8	
9	
10	
11	
12 pm	
1	
2	
3	
4	
5	
6	
7	
8	

Today's Priorities:

To Do List:

Notes:

Friday
September 20th, 2019

6 am	
7	
8	
9	
10	
11	
12 pm	
1	
2	
3	
4	
5	
6	
7	
8	

Today's Priorities:

To Do List:

Notes:

Saturday
September 21st, 2019

Time	
6 am	
7	
8	
9	
10	
11	
12 pm	
1	
2	
3	
4	
5	
6	
7	
8	

Today's Priorities:

To Do List:

Notes:

Sunday

September 22nd, 2019

Time	
6 am	
7	
8	
9	
10	
11	
12 pm	
1	
2	
3	
4	
5	
6	
7	
8	

Today's Priorities:

To Do List:

Notes:

Monday

September 23rd, 2019

6 am	
7	
8	
9	
10	
11	
12 pm	
1	
2	
3	
4	
5	
6	
7	
8	

Today's Priorities:

To Do List:

Notes:

Tuesday
September 24th, 2019

6 am	
7	
8	**Today's Priorities:**
9	
10	
11	
12 pm	
1	**To Do List:**
2	
3	
4	
5	
6	
7	
8	

Notes:

Wednesday
September 25th, 2019

6 am
7
8
9
10
11
12 pm
1
2
3
4
5
6
7
8

Today's Priorities:

To Do List:

Notes:

Thursday
September 26th, 2019

6 am	
7	
8	
9	
10	
11	
12 pm	
1	
2	
3	
4	
5	
6	
7	
8	

Today's Priorities:

To Do List:

Notes:

Friday
September 27th, 2019

6 am	
7	
8	
9	
10	
11	
12 pm	
1	
2	
3	
4	
5	
6	
7	
8	

Today's Priorities:
_____
_____
_____
_____
_____

To Do List:
_____
_____
_____
_____
_____
_____
_____
_____
_____
_____

Notes:
_____
_____
_____
_____

Saturday

September 28th, 2019

6 am	
7	
8	
9	
10	
11	
12 pm	
1	
2	
3	
4	
5	
6	
7	
8	

Today's Priorities:

To Do List:

Notes:

Sunday
September 29th, 2019

Time	
6 am	
7	
8	
9	
10	
11	
12 pm	
1	
2	
3	
4	
5	
6	
7	
8	

Today's Priorities:

To Do List:

Notes:

Monday
September 30th, 2019

Time		
6 am		
7		Today's Priorities:
8		
9		
10		
11		
12 pm		
1		To Do List:
2		
3		
4		
5		
6		
7		
8		

Notes:

Tuesday

October 1st, 2019

- 6 am
- 7
- 8
- 9
- 10
- 11
- 12 pm
- 1
- 2
- 3
- 4
- 5
- 6
- 7
- 8

Today's Priorities:

To Do List:

Notes:

Wednesday

October 2nd, 2019

6 am	
7	
8	
9	
10	
11	
12 pm	
1	
2	
3	
4	
5	
6	
7	
8	

Today's Priorities:

To Do List:

Notes:

Thursday
October 3rd, 2019

Time	
6 am	
7	
8	
9	
10	
11	
12 pm	
1	
2	
3	
4	
5	
6	
7	
8	

Today's Priorities:

To Do List:

Notes:

Friday

October 4th, 2019

6 am	
7	
8	
9	
10	
11	
12 pm	
1	
2	
3	
4	
5	
6	
7	
8	

Today's Priorities:

To Do List:

Notes:

Saturday

October 5th, 2019

6 am	
7	
8	
9	
10	
11	
12 pm	
1	
2	
3	
4	
5	
6	
7	
8	

Today's Priorities:

To Do List:

Notes:

Sunday

October 6th, 2019

6 am	
7	
8	
9	
10	
11	
12 pm	
1	
2	
3	
4	
5	
6	
7	
8	

Today's Priorities:

To Do List:

Notes:

Monday
October 7th, 2019

6 am	
7	
8	
9	
10	
11	
12 pm	
1	
2	
3	
4	
5	
6	
7	
8	

Today's Priorities:
_____
_____
_____
_____
_____

To Do List:
_____
_____
_____
_____
_____
_____
_____
_____
_____

Notes:
_____
_____
_____

Tuesday

October 8th, 2019

6 am	
7	
8	
9	
10	
11	
12 pm	
1	
2	
3	
4	
5	
6	
7	
8	

Today's Priorities:

To Do List:

Notes:

Wednesday

October 9th, 2019

6 am	
7	
8	
9	
10	
11	
12 pm	
1	
2	
3	
4	
5	
6	
7	
8	

Today's Priorities:

To Do List:

Notes:

Thursday

October 10th, 2019

6 am	
7	
8	
9	
10	
11	
12 pm	
1	
2	
3	
4	
5	
6	
7	
8	

Today's Priorities:

To Do List:

Notes:

Friday
October 11th, 2019

6 am	
7	
8	
9	
10	
11	
12 pm	
1	
2	
3	
4	
5	
6	
7	
8	

Today's Priorities:

To Do List:

Notes:

Saturday
October 12th, 2019

6 am	
7	
8	
9	
10	
11	
12 pm	
1	
2	
3	
4	
5	
6	
7	
8	

Today's Priorities:

To Do List:

Notes:

Sunday
October 13th, 2019

6 am	
7	
8	
9	
10	
11	
12 pm	
1	
2	
3	
4	
5	
6	
7	
8	

Today's Priorities:
_____
_____
_____
_____
_____

To Do List:
_____
_____
_____
_____
_____
_____
_____
_____
_____
_____

Notes:
_____
_____
_____

Monday

October 14th, 2019

6 am	
7	
8	
9	
10	
11	
12 pm	
1	
2	
3	
4	
5	
6	
7	
8	

Today's Priorities:
_____
_____
_____
_____
_____

To Do List:
_____
_____
_____
_____
_____
_____
_____
_____
_____
_____

Notes:
_____
_____
_____

Tuesday

October 15th, 2019

6 am
7
8
9
10
11
12 pm
1
2
3
4
5
6
7
8

Notes:

Today's Priorities:

To Do List:

Wednesday

October 16th, 2019

6 am	
7	
8	
9	
10	
11	
12 pm	
1	
2	
3	
4	
5	
6	
7	
8	

Today's Priorities:

To Do List:

Notes:

Thursday

October 17th, 2019

6 am	
7	
8	
9	
10	
11	
12 pm	
1	
2	
3	
4	
5	
6	
7	
8	

Today's Priorities:

To Do List:

Notes:

Friday

October 18th, 2019

6 am	
7	
8	
9	
10	
11	
12 pm	
1	
2	
3	
4	
5	
6	
7	
8	

Today's Priorities:

To Do List:

Notes:

Saturday

October 19th, 2019

6 am	
7	
8	
9	
10	
11	
12 pm	
1	
2	
3	
4	
5	
6	
7	
8	

Today's Priorities:
_____
_____
_____
_____
_____
_____
_____

To Do List:
_____
_____
_____
_____
_____
_____
_____
_____
_____
_____

Notes:
_____
_____
_____
_____

Sunday

October 20th, 2019

Time	
6 am	
7	
8	
9	
10	
11	
12 pm	
1	
2	
3	
4	
5	
6	
7	
8	

Today's Priorities:

To Do List:

Notes:

Monday
October 21st, 2019

- 6 am
- 7
- 8
- 9
- 10
- 11
- 12 pm
- 1
- 2
- 3
- 4
- 5
- 6
- 7
- 8

Today's Priorities:

To Do List:

Notes:

Tuesday

October 22nd, 2019

6 am	
7	
8	
9	
10	
11	
12 pm	
1	
2	
3	
4	
5	
6	
7	
8	

Today's Priorities:

To Do List:

Notes:

Wednesday

October 23rd, 2019

6 am	
7	
8	
9	
10	
11	
12 pm	
1	
2	
3	
4	
5	
6	
7	
8	

Today's Priorities:

To Do List:

Notes:

Thursday

October 24th, 2019

Time	
6 am	
7	
8	
9	
10	
11	
12 pm	
1	
2	
3	
4	
5	
6	
7	
8	

Today's Priorities:

To Do List:

Notes:

Friday
October 25th, 2019

Time	
6 am	
7	
8	
9	
10	
11	
12 pm	
1	
2	
3	
4	
5	
6	
7	
8	

Today's Priorities:
___
___
___
___
___
___
___

To Do List:
___
___
___
___
___
___
___
___
___
___
___
___

Notes:
___
___
___

Saturday
October 26th, 2019

6 am	
7	
8	
9	
10	
11	
12 pm	
1	
2	
3	
4	
5	
6	
7	
8	

Today's Priorities:

To Do List:

Notes:

Sunday
October 27th, 2019

6 am	
7	
8	
9	
10	
11	
12 pm	
1	
2	
3	
4	
5	
6	
7	
8	

Today's Priorities:

To Do List:

Notes:

Monday

October 28th, 2019

Time	
6 am	
7	
8	
9	
10	
11	
12 pm	
1	
2	
3	
4	
5	
6	
7	
8	

Today's Priorities:

To Do List:

Notes:

Tuesday
October 29th, 2019

Time	
6 am	
7	
8	
9	
10	
11	
12 pm	
1	
2	
3	
4	
5	
6	
7	
8	

Today's Priorities:

To Do List:

Notes:

Wednesday

October 30th, 2019

6 am	
7	
8	
9	
10	
11	
12 pm	
1	
2	
3	
4	
5	
6	
7	
8	

Today's Priorities:

To Do List:

Notes:

Thursday
October 31st, 2019

6 am	
7	
8	
9	
10	
11	
12 pm	
1	
2	
3	
4	
5	
6	
7	
8	

Today's Priorities:

To Do List:

Notes:

Friday

November 1st, 2019

6 am	
7	
8	
9	
10	
11	
12 pm	
1	
2	
3	
4	
5	
6	
7	
8	

Today's Priorities:

To Do List:

Notes:

Saturday
November 2nd, 2019

6 am	
7	
8	
9	
10	
11	
12 pm	
1	
2	
3	
4	
5	
6	
7	
8	

Today's Priorities:

To Do List:

Notes:

Sunday

November 3rd, 2019

Time		
6 am		**Today's Priorities:**
7		
8		
9		
10		
11		
12 pm		
1		**To Do List:**
2		
3		
4		
5		
6		
7		
8		

Notes:

Monday
November 4th, 2019

6 am	
7	
8	
9	
10	
11	
12 pm	
1	
2	
3	
4	
5	
6	
7	
8	

Today's Priorities:

To Do List:

Notes:

Tuesday
November 5th, 2019

6 am	
7	
8	
9	
10	
11	
12 pm	
1	
2	
3	
4	
5	
6	
7	
8	

Today's Priorities:

To Do List:

Notes:

Wednesday

November 6th, 2019

Time	
6 am	
7	
8	
9	
10	
11	
12 pm	
1	
2	
3	
4	
5	
6	
7	
8	

Today's Priorities:

To Do List:

Notes:

Thursday
November 7th, 2019

Time	
6 am	
7	
8	
9	
10	
11	
12 pm	
1	
2	
3	
4	
5	
6	
7	
8	

Today's Priorities:

To Do List:

Notes:

Friday

November 8th, 2019

Time	
6 am	
7	
8	
9	
10	
11	
12 pm	
1	
2	
3	
4	
5	
6	
7	
8	

Today's Priorities:

To Do List:

Notes:

Saturday

November 9th, 2019

6 am	
7	
8	
9	
10	
11	
12 pm	
1	
2	
3	
4	
5	
6	
7	
8	

Today's Priorities:

To Do List:

Notes:

Sunday

November 10th, 2019

6 am	
7	
8	
9	
10	
11	
12 pm	
1	
2	
3	
4	
5	
6	
7	
8	

Today's Priorities:

To Do List:

Notes:

Monday

November 11th, 2019

Time	
6 am	
7	
8	
9	
10	
11	
12 pm	
1	
2	
3	
4	
5	
6	
7	
8	

Today's Priorities:

To Do List:

Notes:

Tuesday

November 12th, 2019

6 am	
7	
8	
9	
10	
11	
12 pm	
1	
2	
3	
4	
5	
6	
7	
8	

Today's Priorities:

To Do List:

Notes:

Wednesday

November 13th, 2019

6 am	
7	
8	
9	
10	
11	
12 pm	
1	
2	
3	
4	
5	
6	
7	
8	

Today's Priorities:

To Do List:

Notes:

Thursday
November 14th, 2019

Time	
6 am	
7	
8	
9	
10	
11	
12 pm	
1	
2	
3	
4	
5	
6	
7	
8	

Today's Priorities:

To Do List:

Notes:

Friday

November 15th, 2019

Time	
6 am	
7	
8	
9	
10	
11	
12 pm	
1	
2	
3	
4	
5	
6	
7	
8	

Today's Priorities:

To Do List:

Notes:

Saturday
November 16th, 2019

6 am	
7	
8	
9	
10	
11	
12 pm	
1	
2	
3	
4	
5	
6	
7	
8	

Today's Priorities:

To Do List:

Notes:

Sunday
November 17th, 2019

Time	
6 am	
7	
8	
9	
10	
11	
12 pm	
1	
2	
3	
4	
5	
6	
7	
8	

Today's Priorities:

To Do List:

Notes:

Monday
November 18th, 2019

6 am	
7	
8	
9	
10	
11	
12 pm	
1	
2	
3	
4	
5	
6	
7	
8	

Today's Priorities:
_____
_____
_____
_____
_____

To Do List:
_____
_____
_____
_____
_____
_____
_____
_____

Notes:
_____
_____
_____

Tuesday
November 19th, 2019

6 am	
7	
8	
9	
10	
11	
12 pm	
1	
2	
3	
4	
5	
6	
7	
8	

Today's Priorities:

To Do List:

Notes:

Wednesday

November 20th, 2019

Time	
6 am	
7	
8	
9	
10	
11	
12 pm	
1	
2	
3	
4	
5	
6	
7	
8	

Today's Priorities:

To Do List:

Notes:

Thursday

November 21st, 2019

Time	
6 am	
7	
8	
9	
10	
11	
12 pm	
1	
2	
3	
4	
5	
6	
7	
8	

Today's Priorities:

To Do List:

Notes:

Friday
November 22nd, 2019

Time	
6 am	
7	
8	
9	
10	
11	
12 pm	
1	
2	
3	
4	
5	
6	
7	
8	

Today's Priorities:

To Do List:

Notes:

Saturday

November 23rd, 2019

Time	
6 am	
7	
8	
9	
10	
11	
12 pm	
1	
2	
3	
4	
5	
6	
7	
8	

Today's Priorities:

To Do List:

Notes:

Sunday
November 24th, 2019

6 am	
7	
8	
9	
10	
11	
12 pm	
1	
2	
3	
4	
5	
6	
7	
8	

Today's Priorities:
_____
_____
_____
_____
_____

To Do List:
_____
_____
_____
_____
_____
_____
_____
_____
_____
_____

Notes:
_____
_____
_____
_____

Monday

November 25th, 2019

6 am	
7	
8	
9	
10	
11	
12 pm	
1	
2	
3	
4	
5	
6	
7	
8	

Today's Priorities:

To Do List:

Notes:

Tuesday

November 26th, 2019

6 am	
7	
8	
9	
10	
11	
12 pm	
1	
2	
3	
4	
5	
6	
7	
8	

Today's Priorities:

To Do List:

Notes:

Wednesday

November 27th, 2019

6 am	
7	
8	
9	
10	
11	
12 pm	
1	
2	
3	
4	
5	
6	
7	
8	

Today's Priorities:

To Do List:

Notes:

Thursday
November 28th, 2019

Time	
6 am	
7	
8	
9	
10	
11	
12 pm	
1	
2	
3	
4	
5	
6	
7	
8	

Today's Priorities:

To Do List:

Notes:

Friday
November 29th, 2019

- 6 am
- 7
- 8
- 9
- 10
- 11
- 12 pm
- 1
- 2
- 3
- 4
- 5
- 6
- 7
- 8

Today's Priorities:

To Do List:

Notes:

Saturday

November 30th, 2019

Time	
6 am	
7	
8	
9	
10	
11	
12 pm	
1	
2	
3	
4	
5	
6	
7	
8	

Today's Priorities:

To Do List:

Notes:

Sunday
December 1st, 2019

6 am	
7	
8	
9	
10	
11	
12 pm	
1	
2	
3	
4	
5	
6	
7	
8	

Today's Priorities:

To Do List:

Notes:

Monday

December 2nd, 2019

Time	
6 am	
7	
8	
9	
10	
11	
12 pm	
1	
2	
3	
4	
5	
6	
7	
8	

Today's Priorities:

To Do List:

Notes:

Tuesday

December 3rd, 2019

6 am	
7	
8	
9	
10	
11	
12 pm	
1	
2	
3	
4	
5	
6	
7	
8	

Today's Priorities:

To Do List:

Notes:

Wednesday

December 4th, 2019

Time	
6 am	
7	
8	
9	
10	
11	
12 pm	
1	
2	
3	
4	
5	
6	
7	
8	

Today's Priorities:

To Do List:

Notes:

Thursday
December 5th, 2019

Time	
6 am	
7	
8	
9	
10	
11	
12 pm	
1	
2	
3	
4	
5	
6	
7	
8	

Today's Priorities:

To Do List:

Notes:

Friday
December 6th, 2019

6 am	
7	
8	
9	
10	
11	
12 pm	
1	
2	
3	
4	
5	
6	
7	
8	

Today's Priorities:

To Do List:

Notes:

Saturday

December 7th, 2019

6 am	
7	
8	
9	
10	
11	
12 pm	
1	
2	
3	
4	
5	
6	
7	
8	

Today's Priorities:

To Do List:

Notes:

Sunday
December 8th, 2019

6 am	
7	
8	
9	
10	
11	
12 pm	
1	
2	
3	
4	
5	
6	
7	
8	

Today's Priorities:

To Do List:

Notes:

Monday

December 9th, 2019

6 am	
7	
8	
9	
10	
11	
12 pm	
1	
2	
3	
4	
5	
6	
7	
8	

Today's Priorities:

To Do List:

Notes:

Tuesday
December 10th, 2019

Time	
6 am	
7	
8	
9	
10	
11	
12 pm	
1	
2	
3	
4	
5	
6	
7	
8	

Today's Priorities:

To Do List:

Notes:

Wednesday

December 11th, 2019

Time	
6 am	
7	
8	
9	
10	
11	
12 pm	
1	
2	
3	
4	
5	
6	
7	
8	

Today's Priorities:

To Do List:

Notes:

Thursday

December 12th, 2019

6 am	
7	
8	
9	
10	
11	
12 pm	
1	
2	
3	
4	
5	
6	
7	
8	

Today's Priorities:

To Do List:

Notes:

Friday

December 13th, 2019

Time	
6 am	
7	
8	
9	
10	
11	
12 pm	
1	
2	
3	
4	
5	
6	
7	
8	

Today's Priorities:

To Do List:

Notes:

Saturday
December 14th, 2019

Time	
6 am	
7	
8	
9	
10	
11	
12 pm	
1	
2	
3	
4	
5	
6	
7	
8	

Today's Priorities:
_____
_____
_____
_____
_____
_____

To Do List:
_____
_____
_____
_____
_____
_____
_____
_____
_____

Notes:

Sunday
December 15th, 2019

Time	
6 am	
7	
8	
9	
10	
11	
12 pm	
1	
2	
3	
4	
5	
6	
7	
8	

Today's Priorities:

To Do List:

Notes:

Monday
December 16th, 2019

Time	
6 am	
7	
8	
9	
10	
11	
12 pm	
1	
2	
3	
4	
5	
6	
7	
8	

Today's Priorities:

To Do List:

Notes:

Tuesday

December 17th, 2019

Time	
6 am	
7	
8	
9	
10	
11	
12 pm	
1	
2	
3	
4	
5	
6	
7	
8	

Today's Priorities:

To Do List:

Notes:

Wednesday
December 18th, 2019

Time	
6 am	
7	
8	
9	
10	
11	
12 pm	
1	
2	
3	
4	
5	
6	
7	
8	

Today's Priorities:
_____
_____
_____
_____
_____
_____

To Do List:
_____
_____
_____
_____
_____
_____
_____
_____
_____

Notes:
_____
_____
_____
_____

Thursday

December 19th, 2019

Time	
6 am	
7	
8	
9	
10	
11	
12 pm	
1	
2	
3	
4	
5	
6	
7	
8	

Today's Priorities:

To Do List:

Notes:

Friday

December 20th, 2019

6 am	
7	
8	
9	
10	
11	
12 pm	
1	
2	
3	
4	
5	
6	
7	
8	

Today's Priorities:

To Do List:

Notes:

Saturday
December 21st, 2019

6 am	
7	
8	
9	
10	
11	
12 pm	
1	
2	
3	
4	
5	
6	
7	
8	

Today's Priorities:

To Do List:

Notes:

Sunday
December 22nd, 2019

Time	
6 am	
7	
8	
9	
10	
11	
12 pm	
1	
2	
3	
4	
5	
6	
7	
8	

Today's Priorities:
_____
_____
_____
_____
_____

To Do List:
_____
_____
_____
_____
_____
_____
_____
_____
_____
_____

Notes:
_____
_____
_____

Monday

December 23rd, 2019

6 am	
7	
8	
9	
10	
11	
12 pm	
1	
2	
3	
4	
5	
6	
7	
8	

Today's Priorities:

To Do List:

Notes:

Tuesday
December 24th, 2019

Time	
6 am	
7	
8	
9	
10	
11	
12 pm	
1	
2	
3	
4	
5	
6	
7	
8	

Today's Priorities:

To Do List:

Notes:

Wednesday

December 25th, 2019

Time		
6 am		
7		Today's Priorities:
8		
9		
10		
11		
12 pm		
1		To Do List:
2		
3		
4		
5		
6		
7		
8		

Notes:

Thursday
December 26th, 2019

Time	
6 am	
7	
8	
9	
10	
11	
12 pm	
1	
2	
3	
4	
5	
6	
7	
8	

Today's Priorities:
_____
_____
_____
_____
_____
_____

To Do List:
_____
_____
_____
_____
_____
_____
_____
_____
_____
_____

Notes:
_____
_____
_____
_____

Friday

December 27th, 2019

6 am	
7	
8	
9	
10	
11	
12 pm	
1	
2	
3	
4	
5	
6	
7	
8	

Today's Priorities:

To Do List:

Notes:

Saturday

December 28th, 2019

6 am	
7	
8	
9	
10	
11	
12 pm	
1	
2	
3	
4	
5	
6	
7	
8	

Today's Priorities:
_____
_____
_____
_____
_____

To Do List:
_____
_____
_____
_____
_____
_____
_____
_____
_____
_____

Notes:
_____
_____
_____
_____

Sunday

December 29th, 2019

6 am	
7	
8	
9	
10	
11	
12 pm	
1	
2	
3	
4	
5	
6	
7	
8	

Today's Priorities:

To Do List:

Notes:

Monday
December 30th, 2019

6 am	
7	
8	
9	
10	
11	
12 pm	
1	
2	
3	
4	
5	
6	
7	
8	

Today's Priorities:

To Do List:

Notes:

Tuesday

December 31st, 2019

6 am	
7	
8	
9	
10	
11	
12 pm	
1	
2	
3	
4	
5	
6	
7	
8	

Today's Priorities:

To Do List:

Notes:

www.ingramcontent.com/pod-product-compliance
Lightning Source LLC
Chambersburg PA
CBHW020625220526
45464CB00001B/33